ENIGMA

A Collection of Poems

Liam A. Flin

authorHOUSE®

AuthorHouse™ UK
1663 Liberty Drive
Bloomington, IN 47403 USA
www.authorhouse.co.uk
Phone: 0800.197.4150

Published by AuthorHouse 04/11/2018

ISBN: 978-1-5462-9129-9 (sc)
ISBN: 978-1-5462-9138-1 (e)

Dedicated to my incredible family and friends

The Destiny Collection
Poems for the despairing

The Creationist Collection
Poems for the creative

The Serenity Collection
Poems for the contented

THE DESTINY COLLECTION

Poems for the despairing

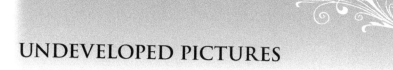

UNDEVELOPED PICTURES

We could have completed the game
of life
together- back then a two-player game.
Now the symphony of forever kisses that we so
intently exchanged
has dried on my cheek.
Words of love and comfort I once
fed you with
are now past expiry,
rotting and decaying in the hung winds
of yesterday.

The path has narrowed, now there's space for only one,
perhaps you were the permanent
passenger
perhaps you will always be in my heart.
The trees now see futility in holding on
and let their leaves depart them,
left bare in the bracing winds
like I am without the coat of you,
the assurance of a future with you
evaporated.

You were the sugar to me,
sweet and enticing but heavily indulgent.
Starved of you, I lack that hyper buzz-
that fuel to lift me out of the bed-sheets.

I have had every hair plucked from my skin
my brainwaves mutilated
and my entire body submerged into a
deep, painful stasis –
inescapable,
and incomprehensible
to the others still playing multiplayer.

Through the night I'm visited by images
new,
These undeveloped pictures of both me and you.

Memories burn like stars, so why don't they fade the same?

HEAL

Under no illusion am I
That the Earth's turn is fast,
days tick by now so slowly.

Prepared for escapism
Assured of advancement
Reality devours like a gorging pig.

You are not allowed to escape
You are not allowed to forget
You are told to learn –
Learn from the mistakes
You did not make
Learn from the afflicted pain.

Amnesia would be a blessing,
Hypnosis a gift,
But you are left with a bow stuck
On top of
A sloppy pile of truth that
You must
Accept
Now.

Nostalgia burns like **inferno**, as I traverse the streets of yesterday.

FLOWERS BY OUR GRAVESTONE

A relationship
pronounced dead at the moment
when you snapped the heart strings.

I visit our gravestone often,
the resting place of the unfinished
the memories we promised to make
have eroded into hot ash
under the natural
cycle of things.

I thought I saw you too,
drifting through the distant foliage,
peaking at our remains,
too afraid of burning to come close
to the site of our end.

A pigeon voraciously pecks at the ground
where our mangled corpse decays.
The flowers by our gravestone
lose petals by the day;
each one an image of the past
dissolved in
the backdrop of my mind.
The vibrancy and beauty of the bunch
when we shared that first kiss
when we walked through the forest of future together,
arms linked then by trust-
it's all withered away now.

Clouds spit down on me in disgust that I still visit,
the only ember still flickering in this
graveyard of broken bonds.
I have let go now
but each day I choose to replenish our
gravestone with flowers new,
a testament to what might have been,
but never will be.

I **embrace** the day when you're my dying ember,

I loathe the day when you're my burning flame.

ABYSS

It is all that she sees.
The endless cascade of black
embeds fragments of purpose
but none substantial enough.

Uncertainty bends the horizon.
This marble earth is too cold
for her warm breath and touch.
Jagged fingernails scratch the surface but she desires a deeper analysis,
a deeper slice of skin.

A girl of former innocence
tainted now by a world of corruption
tainted by a melting pot of indecency around her,
her strong self remains but she cannot see it.

Her life would be reflected on like rose gold mirror, but the outer rim
and bitter end would be dismissed,
until the next little girl grows and sees the globe for what it is, sees the
presence of a future but defies its bloody truth with blade,
plummeting into the abyss.

VOICES

I want impermeable sleep
never again to let people seep
through the pores of my mind
and plant voices in my head.

I am troubled, irrepressibly
by the voices of my past,
silently exploding in brain pockets,
my head is a fortress, bashed in and
invaded.

Yet in the darkest hours of this
clockwork mind,
I feed off my own insecurity.
I devour memories good and bad
as these are reminders of when I actually felt
like I was living.
These voices are my closest
yet most deceitful
friends.

THE WORRIER

That intangible bed of tranquillity has never seemed so far away.
That bed where I lay unfathomed, untouched by daily aggravation and
separate from the consuming, closing fear of concern itself.

Is a worrier not but a warrior who charges into reality with sword ablaze,
accepting that every corner reveals fear and panic?
Am I not the one in the right?

Never does the sickly second hand tick and I not feel repulsed by the
battle that I am to face.
I yearn. I beg. I scream for contentment, not for that buzzing fizz of
happiness which I regularly feel, but a smooth, unbreakable coating of
calm-
I desire a reality that I am not afraid of,
I desire a reality where worry is just a myth.

A good **shower** gets to me,

it washes away the uncertainty.

RAINDROPS

Already I've lost many people
in life.
They are like raindrops
that dribble down the windowpane
elements with both
the nourishing I thirst for
and the interminable soaking
I dread.

They slither ominously
absorbing the beaten sunlight
and reflecting into the back of my mind
to blow the dust off the memories
the avenue where they still live

Some of them turn
rapid
and join together
fragments of the past joining
to form blobs of regret
or reassurances
whilst others shrink and pop
never reaching the bottom of
the pane

Most days it's torrential downpour
and these raindrops
the people of my past
flood the brain
which drowns in the weight of the past
gasping to reach the surface of the present

Other days they're minimal
Whispering against the glass
but extinguished by the heat of now
shrivelled like non-existent raisins
and the pane remains dry
a fresh canvas on which new memories
are sprayed

AGE

My spaniel's chocolate eyes
would once melt by virtue of youthful flames and undefined energy.
Now, the embers barely heat the film of the lens and she withers into
the carpet in front of the fire which man made.

Those paws once knew every inch of soil and grass but now they are
tangled in isolation and tainted by the soft safety-net of time.
Her ears, once fluffed by the kiss of youth, are now flattened by the
weathering weight of continuation, not to mention turbulence.

I hold open her eyelids, anticipating a flashlight of excitement and
energy,
but the dead batteries merely splurge back a blank reply.

DARWIN'S FALSE START

The holy starting gun is fired and
the ants accumulate.
The owls organise.
The gorillas gather-
to them the sun is a tool, no commodity here.
The birds build.
The caribou quickly climb the evolutionary scale.
The doves dive.
The porcupine pricks.
The chameleon croaked but hastily learned to hide.
The wasp showed by hastily learned to sting.

And then,
a helpless human,
he dawdles and withers, for he knew not of constructive gunfire.

DIABLO

That night when the dented
tin cans ran by my feet
and we stood in the street
where you unleashed
the hell of the night and
slit my throat and watched the
evaporated bleeding in your eyes
where I once lived but
that night I learned I would have
to depart. The earth may as well
have split open, mutilating itself,
beneath my feet for I felt no gravity,
I wanted my atoms to disband,
roll like marbles into the crater.
That night you drew perfect plans
from your future, erasing me before
each full stop. You were Krakatoa, fearsome in your pursuit of my
heart, stabbing hard, breaking dark, and feeling the laugh within you,
steaming. You ended me under that lamppost where the darkness began
to pervade and I collapsed and broke down so effortlessly, my small
demon inside, scraping at the eventual carcass with sharp nails and
sinking them deep into the pit of the head, screaming Diablo.

Heaven would have been a place within you, had I not seen the hell before it.

I **bleed** words of destruction. Just don't try sewing me up.

INSPIRED BY DELIRIUM

There's a gap in the walls
of my mind;
the past is a yawning chasm
ever prevalent and twice as dangerous
in its luring of my psyche
in its luring of my future.

A mouth starved of words
means a mind full-to-bursting;
the pregnant mind bursts
with no outlet.

These are caged thoughts that
pace the brainwaves.
I'm ready to quit, I've always been ready.
But
I am told to radiate and craft temporary dreams that will only shatter
like a vase encasing roses of paradise thoughts.

The inside of eyelids reflect back the morose picture of deflated brain
which is eager to be devoured by its past and show the white flag to
the future.
It is a brain whose actions are inspired by delirium.

VILLAINY

I never wanted to assume this role.
I was crammed into the slot and told I would be the villain for this show of life.

My true feelings are so often masked by thick paint to appease the worries of everybody else.

A lifetime of niceties viewed merely as villainy.
I am the maverick
the one time that I look out for myself and all the other moments of heroism and kindness are erased like faded pencil lines.

The moment I am put first, I await the chorus of disapproval from the prepped audience of ignorant.

I only intended to remain a baby cub forever and never inflict pain but the one time I bit back in fear, I was portrayed as the bloodthirsty alpha male, which people just love to depict.

Our hearts were **magnetic poles,** in arguments both sides faced out and repelled. Sometimes we forgot they had other sides.

DESCENT

I am an expert at
extinguishing supernovas;
I killed my spark, dead, now I don't know
what I am.

The demons below don't like my moments of euphoria, the moments
when my heart sings.
When a smile spreads across my face, my heart opens up and my eyes
widen to complete
contentment,
they grapple my feet and hoist me down below
into inescapable black,
where they'll trap me for days.

People ask why I don't visit the earth's surface with smile on face again;
it's because I'm not allowed, the creatures below will take me, perhaps
for even longer
a time.

It's an aurora, an endless cycle of spiralling emotion – never permanently
happy, never permanently sad, just drained empty when the emotion
shows.

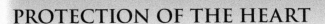

PROTECTION OF THE HEART

Cover the sleeve's enticing edge and you
will not burn, I tell myself.
Suck the heart back in, so it conceals itself under the guardian of flesh.
I become a hooded villain when I enshroud myself and cower cautiously
to efface Cupid's addictive glance.
He aims an arrow in my direction but I burst at my skin's seams to avoid
it; love will be forever painful in a world as greedy and selfish as this.

I have been burned before, you know, even told it was my fault, told my
thick catalogue of errors over time sparked the collapse.
I gave my heart away like putty in sweaty hands, malleable to any
extent, strings were snapped and the righteous red deflated and now
my heart is blue. It is in a coma, a deep sleep, not wanting of another
female's touch, for fear she'll awaken it too soon.
Never again will they be let in without the password of knowing how
not to break lonely hearts.

In poetry it doesn't matter if you're broken, it's not writing to put you back together, it's writing about the **pieces** that have fallen apart.

INFERIOR

I feel as though I was
Born inferior.
These demonic whispers
Are grappling at me
Tantalising
And telling me I'm no good.
My skin is paler than his,
My teeth more jagged
And my muscles pathetic.
You
You
You
Are an excuse of a man
Pathetic and worthless
This unrelenting drumbeat rolls on
Earthquakes in the mind
Causing me to shudder
Inside out.

This skin is sticky and uncomfortable
I don't like it
I don't like me.
Flooded by cowardice
Hung up and obsessive over a false image
I'm still failing to get it right.
Can I be someone else now please?

It's forgetting **yesterday** that's so hard.

CLINGING TO PURPOSE

You were how I woke up,
my invaded thoughts,
pulsating and vivid,
my literal lifeblood,
lavishing me with essence,
the flowing sap to my aged tree,
the dilating diesel to my sports car,
how I imagined those future years.
You were those future years,
my reason of being
my purpose evolved
a raging forest fire
intent on devouring my passions.
You were my passions.
You were every thought of mine
Every fizzle in the nerves
the valiant wings of birds
the track beneath the train
keeping me on course.
In my mind you still reside
but I always forget
you even played
these
roles for me.

I am **magnetic** to doomsday.

WRITING AT 2AM

I've been told
I melt
when I love.
Those chemicals, they do things
to me,
tap into my consciousness
and tell it to
awaken me
and lend itself to someone
new.

I grab a jug and
pour myself
into the new feature,
she has all of me,
I fall fast, perhaps
too fast.

Heart so far up
my sleeve that
it drops off the end
and squelches on the floor.
I hope this time it doesn't get used to mop up mess from night before.

SNOWFALL

I see you in the icicles,
Hanging so perfectly that you're in my eyeline again.
Each snowflake is a different mood of yours, a different identity you
freeze into.

This is a reflection of time, weighted. I am myself long in summer
where the river runs fluid but you loved the rigid core of winter, where
everything stays the same, every moment encased for a lifetime.

I argue with my brain which season it is; in my heart I want it to be
summer but the cold winds tell me that it is long away. Moving on is a
challenge, but one to enjoy.

Now it's clear what it's all about; these flakes of former friends that drift,
these flakes I should stick my heated tongue out towards and absorb; I
should be constructed of the people I have
crossed
Before.

I should let the snow fall because
It's natural and I need to be showered with my past, showered with a
winter's frost if I am ever to fully appreciate the rebirth of earth
in spring.

FRAGMENTS

Decipher the fragments and put me back together;
I was shattered by love and lost myself.

The watercolour heart spilled out
and
tried
to find the excuses to
glue the pieces back together.

Now though I accept
I
Accept
That these fragments belong
To you
a lost love
our memories were solidified
and
broke from
me
the belongings of the past
maybe post them back
to me
one day.

DESTINY

In this forest of thought I find myself,
Contemplating the ultimate purpose,
Ravenous for answers I tear down walls
Of bromeliad and orchid beneath,
Until Arcadia peers through at me.
A silky stream sparkles like diadem,
Restricting rallying piranha croak
and stealing beams that shine overhead.
The ears are treated to a soft chorus,
The eyes are tantalised by vast colour
And the bountiful promises offered;
The indulgence and endless fuel of cocoa,
The indefinite nutrition of banana plant,
The eternal life exhaled by wimba,
All assured certainties on the other side.

I am buoyant on the water lilies,
Guided by my weightless psyche across,
Across to the ultimate portal,
Which no man dares to question or face.
Destiny, you've been a villain to me,
Yet now I shall see through the façade
and will uncover what jewels await me
and unveil the immutable truth.
As the waterfall runs intimately,
Caressing curved rock so effortlessly,
I grab a pocket of air with bottom lip

And violently inhale to control my
essence,
Across enemy lines I will transcend,
Out of the world of not knowing,
And into the world of certainty
To procure the truth of destiny.

Under the flurry of water things change.
Through nature's silky window of future,
Hopes of wealth and health fade and
Dissipate,
Leaving just ash and dust and
Armageddon.
It seems painfully evident now that
the man who tries to pursue his dreams,
Before Mother Nature explains what they are,
Will be left with none and with this destiny
Relinquished,
His potential is but eroded rock and the exit is blocked
By the flowing tears of his
former self.

THE CREATIONIST COLLECTION

Poems for the creative

FOR THE LOVE OF POETRY

As each word trickles onto
the page
warmth strikes me at my core
each letter a symbol of
raw emotion
yet to be explained and unfathomed,
the breeding ground of
thought and feeling
to write is to get intimate
with language
the romance of the tongue
these letters I grasp under the
moonlight
and take them to dinner
analyse and explore them
until we fall into each other's arms
and together form what is
beauty in my mind
and raw words ready to be
absorbed by my brethren.

HUNT

Ethereal glider through the trees,
Menacing in the snow,
A creature I have longed for,
A creature I yearn to know.

The trees straddle over blanket,
Obstacles in my pursuit,
You tease me in the distance,
You make the world fall mute.

Bracing winds cause overlap,
As you, creature, in the shadows dance,
Deceptively, enticingly,
My art you will enhance.

Then I catch your outline.
Your image, it grows stronger,
Snow prints now solidify,
Hunt won't last much longer.

Sprinting and gasping,
I chase you through bitter cold,
Snowy pathways like sugar icing,
That is decaying, rotting, old.

You are golden to me,
Something so rare and great to catch,
Every writer wants you,
A chance at which they'd snatch.

I fire a bullet through your neck,
A bullet of desire,
I have caught you now softly,
You fuel to my fire.

That night I feed on your carcass,
A carcass of intellectual sensation,
You are not physical, just an element of mind,
I have found you at last, you, my inspiration.

That night I wrote and wrote and wrote, until I no longer held the **pen**, but the pen held me.

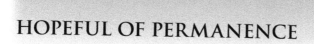

HOPEFUL OF PERMANENCE

Language is full transcendence,
an imprint in the concrete,
untouched by the erosion of time.

The hairs on my head lighten,
blood cools around withered organs,
yet mind and memory churn out words.

My voice is passed like baton,
generations feel like me,
my heartache, love, joy and happiness.

Those memories I enclosed,
A bold, permanent life-span,
ineffaceable to everyone.

This is no arrogance, no,
this is contentment now fuelled,
fuelled by the rattle of a keyboard.

Certainty is just old myth,
but not in the writer's world,
where all words placed are immovable.

Every word has **power** in the hands of the right poet.

The **tragedy** of the writer is being unable to live in the worlds they create.

MIND-MAZE

The translucent eyes reveal a chaotic mind, in which anything is possible.

Neurones charged with the blood of a bull,
stampeding fiery against the magma sky,
fuelled by anger, ready to initiate shockwaves,
ready to hit fight over flight, raging and developing,
developing now into a curious cub stunned by fear.

It shrinks and it shrinks and it shrinks, cowering into the cracked walls
of the brain, enshrouding itself in the blankets of nerve-endings,
where it peers through the eyes of the head and sees inevitable danger
in every corner,
it sees curtain rails as domestic weapons eager to destroy,
it sees the bath mat as a stingray eager to devour,
it sees plug-holes as portals to an inescapable purgatory.
Navigating the crevices of the mind-maze, the former bull and cub is
now metamorphosed into a creature of sorrow, twisting, amalgamating,
spinning and shrinking yet again.

This creature bursts its vessels and hangs its head now as a solemn sloth,
plagued with sadness and uncertainty.
Its desire drops.
Confusion sets in.
Futility is all it sees now.
The skin visible through the futile lenses is just a casing for a mutable form.
The nails are there to grow and then be cut away like yesterday's news.

The feet are liars dedicated to holding up a corpse that will never live eternally.
The legs are just as bad and the arms that extend out are the perpetrators of continuous, unforgiveable bad.

Now it seems that times of anger, anxiety and sorrow are distant memories as the brain hits red alert and this creature assumes its new and most powerful form of all.

The fur of the former bull is loosened to a calming coat of determination, the cub's innocence is the required blissful naivety and the slowness of the sloth is but careful consideration;
all are ingredients to concoct the being that breaks down the walls of the maze and creates;
this is the artist of the mind, a being forever woken by experience bad and good, who feeds off life.
The artist is ready to create, the mind-maze has been navigated and the masterpiece is already nearly complete.

The **beauty** of being a poet is that everything you experience, no matter how painful, fuels the thing you love most of all.

I was kept awake last night by whispers of my **utopia.**

CENTRE STAGE

I don't want centre stage; it's reserved for my words.
They dance and sing, joke and provoke and the audience are mesmerised by them.
I like it that way; I am the inconspicuous director, orchestrating beauty from behind the curtain.

WHO?

Who is this boy so keen to spill his guts onto the page for analysis, so ignorant of poetic rule and mindless of meter?

Who is this child exploding words like chemistry, accessing linguistic weaponry without the experience to handle it?

Who is this teen so intent on outdating himself with a fumbling rhythmic flow, so intent on ruining poetry?

Who is this young man scrambling with words in the night, not in clubs or pubs or bars, instead torturing himself with the pen against the backdrop of frowns and laughter?

Who? I'll tell you who. This man is addicted. Addicted to outflow of emotion, obsessed with curves of the letters and infatuated, he invests love into poetry and one day, maybe, that will be reciprocated.

NOTEBOOK OF THOUGHTS

The black lake has burst
I take the notebook of thoughts
And begin outpour

Times of good and bad
Are funnelled onto the lines
Concrete emotion

Darkened marmalade
Of a heart broken and used
Inks the nub of pen

Then moments of love
Kindness and jubilation
Spill out of the end

Here in this notebook
I will write the messages
Sent from the above

I take no credit
For words that fell from the sky
And became my life

Poet is translator
Translator between two worlds
Of here and above

These notebook pages
Canvas of experience
Ready for next verse

Writing is not my passion, it's my **identity**.

LOVE LETTER TO WORDS

When there's nobody left to turn to,
When I don't want to aggravate more mortal souls,
You still remain
My strongest forever option.
Words, I cannot thank you enough for your service.
I use you to transmit broken thoughts
I use you to deflect unfriendly memories.
Most of
All
I use you to escape and you neutralise
Everything.

Each
Scratch of pen
Each
Tap of keyboard
Is like thought flowing out and morphine flowing in, a heavy calming
of the buzz of feeling. You make logic of man's demise.

I strip myself down to bare bones and layer strips of myself onto the
page but each letter cradles them gently; I'm in good hands with you.

Words,
I love you, dearly and solemnly, you never hurt me if you're in my grasp,
you'd never destroy, you just give me the
Power to do
so.

Cherish your words like new-borns, they're fresh off your tongue.

HOW THE WORDS WORK

I always thought
that words were
for good people only-
only those with the delicate
palms, sensual, smooth and soft,
could cradle such sweet delights
of language.

As I grew up
I saw these little words grow too,
grow through experience.
They were battered in the playground,
Thrown against the walls.
They were strangled and beaten, a vulgar pulp squeezed out by the linguistic
bully, fumbling phrases.

I saw words sat across the street,
traipsing through wet exclamation marks
with their umbrellas stolen
and their clothing torn.

I saw big words stretched so far
rapidly wrung out and
left
to dribble out dissolved meaning.

I saw two people, walking their words to school-
a man scrunching his fist round the hand of his words, unequivocally uncaring,
he drains them of their essence, a random spat of language blows up like a flurry, meaning lost in a thunderstorm of the blithering idiot.
He throws his words through the school gates, forgetting their names, confusing adjective for noun, adverb for verb, he tells them not to come home, he has used them now.
Another woman sits down with her words before the school day dawns, tells them what is what and how to behave. She strokes the cheeks of the little connective, kisses the pronoun on its head and nudges them lovingly towards the gates to begin the day.

The alarm bells sound and the words jiggle. Two teachers watch these words assemble and before long they heap praise on the words of the man,
so broken and misused,
but completely blank the woman's little words, they're too constructed.

Now I know words are not for good people
only-
they're at the disposal of all,
taken and accepted by everyone,
regardless of upbringing.

Nights have been lost through my many fights with words.

OFFICE POET

Through the window
The sky turns from
Its midnight blue
And the workers
Roll in through the doors,
A monotonous mess.

Lines and lines and lines
And lines and lines
Of pressed suits shape
Voiceless ghosts
Who rattle keyboards
With numb fingers and a jaw
Forced open intermittently
By the daybreak yawns.

Crumpled paper grey and miserable
A minefield of mundanity
Spread across office floor.
The telephone buzz is muted itself
By the cold chorus of boredom.

Raindrops once clear and
Crystallised
Hang grey and opaque on the window
Pane
Solidified by the office clock
That threatens to go backwards.

Lunchtime sandwiches
The same every day
In sealed translucent bags
Atoms of the outside packed away.

One man sits hunched in the corner,
His head swung away from the dissolving screen
And he sits staring out
The window at city skyline
And amalgamation of colour
In its backdrop so vivid.

He's the dreamer today;
These features tap dance in his mind
Sizzling with such passion.
He unscrunches paper aeroplane
And scribbles word fragments
Along the wings,
Throws it out the window and
Hopes for better things.

This is the Office Poet
He is all that we are
Humanity so hung up on work
And money
And the devil of pragmatism
We are all artists, trapped in a world
Failing the vision
Trapped in a world of workers.

Please let me be **remembered** by the words that came to me.

We all need a bit of poetic **release**.

CREATIONIST

The fibres twitch and spring into action, connecting the crackling cranium to a pulse of creativity.

As the writer now born learns to walk without earth's fine roots locked to their feet, learns to sing without the nightingale locked in their heart, learns to breathe without the supply of the winds.

The grass below and the sky above are now part of a pallet in the midst of growth, a linguistic love the paintbrush and every speck of creation the paint;

this is the heart of a writer but never will the eternal footprint left behind appeal to them as it will the audience.

THE SERENITY COLLECTION

Poems for the contented

REGENERATION

You can deceive me,
You can destroy me,
You can hurt me,
But you'll never end me.

Now
Is the time for
Rebuild;
Rebuild
I will.

Undone by deception and dishonest reflection the game is over but I
will play again, perhaps alone to learn the rules.

The outside is a breaking dawn and I'm a wreck
A crumbling mess
With an apology taped to my Face
But the core pulses with
Confidence
At my heart I am strong
And soon the beast of rebirth
Is to
Be
Unleashed.

RAIN CLOUD

If she ever appears a rain cloud,
Let her rain down on you.
Let her every insecurity drown your pores.
To battle her rain with the sunlight of acceptance is to create a rainbow

Of love

And that

Is a beautiful

Concoction.

The most attractive quality of all is the presence of your **future** in their eyes; an undeniable protection of that future. Nothing beats that.

She **redefines** beauty.

ETERNAL

Allow me to bellow whispers of your perfection
and borrow your mind, your secrecies, your voice and your dreams as
this is the world where you can do wrong but will always be forgiven
this is the world of my own mind and here you lay down on scented grass
surrounded by ethereal trees and blushing sunlight, but you remain the
most divine essence of this sweet earth.

FOR LOVE

For every freckle on her face,
adore an imperfection,
she radiates enigmatically in your presence,
you're the fuel of her soul.

Indulge in his crooked smile and poorly shaven cheeks,
his mismatched clothes,
and disintegrating abs.
He loves it when you look at him
that way
with a harmony in your gaze,
appreciating all that is wrong
and right
within him.

Even in arguments
the words fizzle between you
and that
is a feeling to fight for.
An undeniable passion
reinforced
by acceptance of flaws.

You wanted champagne
and he's just lemonade
but he's much sweeter
and who needs intoxication
when you're drunk on his love.

He gazes at him,
she gazes at her,
she gazes at him,
unbounded love,
you gaze at each other
under the duvet, not the stars,
simplicity sets in and you
both
think,
'darling, you put the hopeful in
romantic'.

Make her your **Enigma,** not to be worked out, but to be gazed at with a fond mystification.

I'm just a **hopeful** romantic, clinging to those stars, the ones yet to be born.

Love is our celebration of **imperfections**.

RADIANCE

The dead folds of winter are peeled back and beams emerge radiant and new,
now there's energy deep within me, harnessed from the hard times I got through.

The aromas of the air are changing with a pale blue above suffocating the darkness, gone are my looming pitfalls of uncertainty,
gone are those extendable days of helpless.

This is a world of radiance, something beautiful and bright,
the earth is a new-born, stumbling fresh.
We are all still learning about advance and demise, we are all still scrambling for permanent beauty in this mess.

On this spring day the blending of seasons is sweet,
fragrant flavours for all the senses, it's a cold but not bitter wind,
my hair beats back in the breeze and my skin is sore, but this is the natural cleansing of the earth and thus something I desire forever more.

Boldly I step into the vortex they said was too risky,
I emerge from simplicity to embrace challenge,
In the same way the caterpillars metamorphose into creatures of flight on which their fate does hinge.

SHIFT

I forgot who I am.
Strengths and weaknesses alike
Dissolved
In a blinded pallet.
It's time.
It's time to change.
It's time to grow.
Life has caught up and is
Now fully charged.
I am energised
Energised
Like
Radioactive dynamo.
Self-unity
Self-Strength
Self-Motivation.
This era is the era
Of self
The era
Of me.

Travel, engage, work
Play, explore, determine, love, hate, miss, regret, sob, rebuild, strengthen
And live.

The day is done but time
Will not crumble
Time is about to
Shift.

ON FIRST TASTING LOVE

They say that you broke me, ended me,
scolded me out of impermanence.
They call you the serpent who deceived me even though I'd felt the
pump of poison many times by you before.
They named you the perilous teardrop, drifting in the ocean of woe.
They pronounced you a mistake to be etched out in bloodthirsty rage,
a repulsive stain to be scratched and rubbed out. You are supposed to
repulse me,

but,

you were my first love.
We trod waters turbulent and vast,
never really wanting to relinquish that grasp we had of one another.
At the end we were too scared to go under depths.

I sat in your classroom,
beady-eyed and ready to learn about love. You taught me
taught me of the perils and wonders of that four lettered cosmos.
Silence
would do our beautiful bond better justice than my words ever will do,
times which were almost too good.

I drag the words out of me now like daggers from a wound,
painful to approach,
painful to remember,
but delicate and wondrous nonetheless.

Never had I felt so close to another
than when I held you in my arms
on winter nights, in sweet stasis we sat,
reconciling those future thoughts
that fuzzed in our minds.
On summer afternoons, the clock would tick but time was endless-
A sky of pulsating possibility.
We were bare. We were untouchable.

You gave me those fairy-tale memories
baked in the magenta summer sky.
We were grapes on the vine,
so nourishing but perhaps destined
to lose all sweetness.

My first love,
you taught me heartache and to appreciate
that
what we had was before its time,
magnificent
and simply bloody brilliant.

First love,
I forgive you forever
and can never be bitter.

You taught me in that classroom
love's fair mutability
and now I will cherish it
all the more.

WEEDS WILL ALWAYS GROW

Weeds will always grow
And spoil the flowers.
Clouds will always gather
And obstruct the light.
Leaves will always wither
And take summer with them.

Just a tick-tock on the eternal clock
And such damage is undone by the growth of beauty,
The roar of nourishment and
Before long these lonely days are
Forgotten; but the innocent dead never will
Be.

Warped, cowardly killers will always act
Repulsively,
But their isolation is nothing to our
Triumphant love and unity.

IN APPRECIATION

In appreciating the new-born naivety of
fresh wind waves,
You will find happiness.

In appreciating the unity of the snow packed tightly,
You will find happiness.

In appreciating the freedom and naked expression of trees stripped bare,
You will find happiness.

In appreciating the barnstorming determination of nature to survive,
You will find happiness.

In appreciating the way the globe relaxes still in the winter's frost,
You will find happiness.

Winter is not a sad summer, it's just purer feeling and in finding the
intricate delicacies of the world so appealing,
Happiness will find you.

WRITING TO MYSELF

You are going to cry
You are going to punch
You are going to erupt,
You are going to burn inside,
A gooey molten mess.

Sickness will be commonplace,
Desolation a mere headache,
You are going to scream,
You are going to die
Inside.
You are going to hate, hate, hate
You are going to love, love, love
But
You are going to be strong
Because
The best things in life haven't happened
Yet.
Keep going.

INDIGO

Here in my dreams I see it so,
A calming world of indigo.

Origami hearts shatterproof,
A world dictated by love and truth.

Where weather bends round your feeling,
Undisturbed globe, prepped for healing.

World of unbroken melody,
World of promise, just wait and see.

Soundtrack of sweet and fine bird song,
Where everyone knows right from wrong.

No questions, strife or arguments,
World in balance, it all makes sense.

That's why we link **passions** to fire – what we love can burn us to our cores in our darkest hours, but also ignite a whirlwind in the soul.

I want to be the **flash** of light in someone's darkening storm.

NEW AGE

Let that time of year consume the air, as does its guardian, the sun, fill my room and softly awaken me in March.

The dreary, hanging tree fingers are now clothed with blossom and greenery swarms the pale concrete.
Silenced no more are the delicate harmonies of birds and blind no more are we to the millions upon millions of tiny friends, which have manifested in the bushes.

Whispering narcissi restore the drained chambers of life; each petal absolves the body from winter's damage and cradles us into the heightened heat of summer.

MOON OF HONEY

Always the same, whoever it is, but we
forget
that
so intentionally.

They are new, they are fresh. They make our hearts pulse to the size of
pomegranates
this is the beginning
when sweetness is the flavour
that floods the mouth so dear,
a time of fresh adventure
where faded love grows near.

They are the moon of honey
a new beginning hung in starlight
you look up at them and realise that
you wasted time on stars
impermanent
burning
when the stable
honey moon was always
possible.

Wild sex and dinner dates were the products of their passion; **cold nights cuddling** were the creators.

In that **smile** of hers you see a million complications, all woven together into one big simplicity.

OVERCOMPLICATE

I tried to overcomplicate her but she's as simple as can be;
Beauty that transcends the skin, layered inside and out, a warm radiance
unseen before and a glorious danger that just says, come and look at
how I see the world.

BOND OF OLD

To that care home she came
every day
to ignite that bond of old.

Her mute words would spill out
onto his lap
he sits arched in that chair,
an outlier from reality,
any straggles of youth flaking away.

An affection like
green apple slices
carved them into one form.

LIVING FOR A SECOND TIME

I shed away the skin of yesterday,
unbearable,
shed it back and I peer through
to a dimension
fragrant and different.

I've been under the sand for so long
addicted to desolation
but today I've been watered
pure and fresh.

I breath in life's wonders now,
anticipating, exhaling,
reimagining
the streamlined corridor I've been fixed
upon
now to investigate the rooms,
a world open and ready.

Let me dive
dive dive
right into the whirlpools of
blistering uncertainty
and let me steal steal
steal
these bubbles

let me be the current
energetic and vibrant.

My life is building blocks
and I've just taken a sledgehammer
to them
not hung up on vertigo
I'm looking up up up
I'm seeing skyscraper living
full of endless experimentation
skyscrapers
unbounded and pristine.

Something has grabbed me
Something has shaken me
rattles my heart heart heart
now it's unchained itself and bent the bars
of this ramshackle prison
destroyed and reborn.

There are skeletons tucked in the back of
the wardrobe but I will stand face-on to
them no more
I shut the door
and let the key
plunge

into oblivion
they are still there but
they will disintegrate in my mind's
purgatory
dismembered and dying.

This is the eureka of the mind
and we are all in pursuit of its intermittent
flashes
so I tell you, grab the beams, grab them, grab them
and start living
again.

That kiss they shared was an imprint; a **tattoo** of promise never to leave their lips.

Stories yet to be written are the best kind.

THE GOOD KIND OF CARELESS

And that day I wandered along
naked feet free from the trouser cut
hair unbrushed and fluffed
a gleaming remainder of sleep
in my eyes.

Shirts baggy and creased drowned
my torso
there was an elemental breeze
brewing in my heart
an upbeat pitter-patter of rain rumbling
fresh and smooth
in my ear drum.

The water of the rain rolled off and nourished me from head to toe
it was sunny every day now in my mind.

The background confined conflict,
hate and deceit,
the foreground bulged and split with
happy thought
contentment cut through
and grass grew
rapidly and fast
the food of the focused.

I'm just **happy** speculating the many ways that life could go.

FAMILIARITY

It's you I love so dear
Familiarity.
How you smooth the sharp harsh edges of
Reality.
How you drain the fear and dread right out of me.
How you lighten bated breath so
Easily.
How you let this cold mind feel so
Free.
You're the radiator smile that just lets me
Be.
You're an outlet even better than my
Poetry.

Can't you see it?
It is she,
Who's my familiarity.

You can see it in her, **indents** of the past and promises for the future.

FLOW

Doors behind my forehead
swing open
unhinged and liberated
as the flow of thought
unleashes itself
and begins travelling
to the numbed regions of
my body
energising, illuminating, enriching
these organs
with emotion
fresh out of the oven
piping hot and so daringly
real
it floods my veins
but they do not burn
this passion's heat
revitalises the nerves
and elevates the inner soul
and outer body
one unit
uplifted and given the nutrition of pure human feeling
the regular beat of pain
the rapid rhythm of love
the crackling crescendo of loss
all pump and pump

through these roots
of the soul
all I hope will just
evaporate from my skin's surface
no longer my own problem
but the discussion of
the world.

Everyone after **success** needs that voice telling them they can't do it.

SERENITY

The art of everything;
Master it to become
Undefeated by life.

Pearls of wisdom
Shatterproof
When you just accept the truth.

Change is not an action
Beheld by humanity
But a state of being
The most powerful force
In existence

To overcome this
Demon of darkness
Enigma of ambiguity
Just breath
Just accept
Just recognise
That serenity
Is your
Antidote.